Wanted—A Ma

Paul Leicester Ford

Alpha Editions

This edition published in 2024

ISBN 9789362994684

Design and Setting By
Alpha Editions
www.alphaedis.com
Email - info@alphaedis.com

As per information held with us this book is in Public Domain.
This book is a reproduction of an important historical work.
Alpha Editions uses the best technology to reproduce historical work
in the same manner it was first published to preserve its original nature.
Any marks or number seen are left intentionally to preserve.

Wanted: A Match-Maker

"You understand, Josie, that I wouldn't for a moment wish Constance to marry without being in love, but—"

Mrs. Durant hesitated long enough to convey the inference that she was unfeminine enough to place a value on her own words, and then, the pause having led to a change, or, at least, modification of what had almost found utterance, she continued, with a touch of petulance which suggested that the general principle had in the mind of the speaker a special application, "It is certainly a great pity that the modern girl should be so unimpressionable!"

"I understand and sympathise with you perfectly, dear," consolingly acceded Mrs. Ferguson. "And Constance has such advantages!"

Quite unnoting that her friend replied to her thought rather than to her words, Mrs. Durant responded at once eagerly, yet defensively: "That is it. No one will deny that Muriel is quite Constance's equal in mind, and, though perhaps I am not the one to say it, Doris surely excels her in looks. Don't you think so, darling?" she added.

"Unquestionably," agreed the friend, with much the quality of firm promptness with which one would bolt a nauseous pill, or extrude an ailing oyster.

"Yet merely because Constance has been out so much longer, and therefore is much more experienced, she self—she monopolises the attentions of the men; you know she does, Josie."

"Absolutely," once more concurred Mrs. Ferguson; and this time, though she spoke less quickly, her tone carried greater conviction. "They are— well—she—she undoubtedly—that is, she contrives—somehow—to eclipse, or at least overshadow them."

"Exactly. I don't like to think that she manages—but whether she does or not, the results are as bad as if she did; and thoughtlessness—if it is only that, which I can't believe—is quite as blamable as—as more intentional scheming."

"Then of course," said Mrs. Ferguson, "every one knows about her mother's fortune—and men are so mercenary in these days."

"Oh, Josie, I don't like to speak of that myself, but it is such a relief to have you say it. That is the whole trouble. What sort of a chance have my poor dears, who will inherit so little compared to her wealth, and that not till—till we are through with it—against Constance? I call it really shameful of her to keep on standing in their light!"

"Have you—Couldn't you let her see—drop a hint—of the unconscious injury she is—"

"That is the cruelty of my position," moaned Mrs. Durant. "I should not hesitate a moment, but the world is so ill-natured about stepmothers that one has to be over-careful, and with daughters of my own, I'm afraid people—perhaps my own husband—would think I was trying to sacrifice her to them."

"But have you no friend you could ask to—?"

"Josie! Would you?" eagerly interrupted Mrs. Durant. "She will be influenced, I know, by anything you—"

"Gracious, my dear, I never dreamed of—of you asking me! Why, I don't know her in the least. I couldn't, really."

"But for my sake? And you know her as well as—as any one else; for Constance has no intimates or—"

"Don't you see that's it? I'd as soon think of—of—From me she would only take it as an impertinence."

"I don't see why everybody stands so in awe of a girl of twenty-three, unless it's because she's rich," querulously sighed Mrs. Durant.

"I don't think it's that, Anne. It's her proud face and reserved manner. And I believe those are the real reasons for her not marrying. However much men may admire her, they—they—Well, it's your kittenish, cuddling kind of a girl they marry."

"No; you are entirely wrong. Doubtless it is her money, but Constance has had plenty of admirers, and if she were less self—if she considered the interests of the family—she would have married years ago. But she is wholly blind to her duty, and checks or rebuffs every man who attempts to show her devotion. And just because others take their places, she is puffed up into the belief that she is to go through life with an everlasting train of would-be suitors, and so enjoys her own triumph, with never a thought of my girls."

"Why not ask her father to speak to her?"

"My dear! As if I hadn't, a dozen times at the least,"

"And what does he say?"

"That Constance shows her sense by not caring for the men *I* invite to the house! As if *I* could help it! Of course with three girls in the house one must cultivate dancing-men, and it's very unfair to blame me if they aren't all one could wish."

"I thought Constance gave up going to dances last winter?"

"She did, but still I must ask them to my dinners, for if I don't they won't show Muriel and Doris attention. Mr. Durant should realise that I only do it for their sakes; yet to listen to him you'd suppose it was my duty to close my doors to dancing-men, and spend my time seeking out the kind one never hears of—who certainly don't know how to dance, and who would either not talk at my dinners, or would lecture upon one subject to the whole table—just because they are what he calls 'purposeful men.'"

"He probably recognises that the society man is not a marrying species, while the other is."

"But there are several who would marry Constance in a minute if she'd only give any one of them the smallest encouragement; and that's what I mean when I complain of her being so unimpressionable. Muriel and Doris like our set of men well enough, and I don't see what right she has to be so over-particular."

Mrs. Ferguson rose and began the adjustment of her wrap, while saying, "It seems to me there is but one thing for you to do, Anne."

"What?" eagerly questioned Mrs. Durant.

"Indulge in a little judicious matchmaking," suggested the friend, as she held out her hand.

"It's utterly useless, Josie. I've tried again and again, and every time have only done harm."

"How?"

"She won't—she is so suspicious. Now, last winter, Weston Curtis was sending her flowers and—and, oh, all that sort of thing, and so I invited him to dinner several times, and always put him next Constance, and tried to help him in other ways, until she—well, what do you think that girl did?"

Mrs. Ferguson's interest led her to drop her outstretched hand. "Requested you not to?" she asked.

"Not one word did she have the grace to say to me, Josie, but she wrote to him, and asked him not to send her any more flowers! Just think of it."

"Then that's why he went to India."

"Yes. Of course if she had come and told me she didn't care for him, I never would have kept on inviting him; but she is so secretive it is impossible to tell what she is thinking about. I never dreamed that she was conscious that I was trying to—to help her; and I have always been so discreet that I think she never would have been if Mr. Durant hadn't begun to joke about it. Only guess, darling, what he said to me once right before her, just as I thought I was getting her interested in young Schenck!"

"I can't imagine."

"Oh, it was some of his Wall Street talk about promoters of trusts always securing options on the properties to be taken in, before attempting a consolidation, or something of that sort. I shouldn't have known what he meant if the boys hadn't laughed and looked at Constance. And then Jack made matters worse by saying that my interest would be satisfied with common stock, but Constance would only accept preferred for hers. Men do blurt things out so—and yet they assert that we women haven't tongue discretion. No, dear, with them about it's perfectly useless for me to do so much as lift a finger to marry Constance off, let alone her own naturally distrustful nature."

"Well, then, can't you get some one to do it for you—some friend of hers?"

"I don't believe there is a person in the world who could influence Constance as regards marriage," moaned Mrs. Durant. "Don't think that I want to sacrifice her, dear; but she really isn't happy herself—for—well— she is a stepdaughter, you know—and so can never quite be the same in the family life; and now that she has tired of society, she really doesn't find enough to do to keep busy. Constance wanted to go into the Settlement work, but her father wouldn't hear of it—and really, Josie, every one would be happier and better if she only would marry—"

"I beg your pardon for interrupting you, mama. I thought you were alone," came a voice from the doorway. "How do you do, Mrs. Ferguson?"

"Oh!" ejaculated both ladies, as they looked up, to find standing in the doorway a handsome girl, with clear-cut patrician features, and an erect carriage which gave her an air of marked distinction.

"I only stopped to ask about the errand you asked me to do when I went out," explained the girl, quietly, as the two women hunted for something to say.

"Oh. Yes. Thank you for remembering, darling," stammered Mrs. Durant, finding her voice at last. "Won't you please order a bunch of something sent to Miss Porter—and—and—I'll be very much obliged if you'll attend to it, Constance, my dear."

The girl merely nodded her head as she disappeared, but neither woman spoke till the front door was heard to close, when Mrs. Durant exclaimed, "How long had she been standing there?"

"I don't know."

"I hope she didn't hear!"

"I don't think she could have, or she would have shown it more,"

"That doesn't mean anything. She never shows anything outwardly. And really, though I wouldn't purposely have said it to her, I'm not sure that I hope she didn't hear it—for—well, I do wish some one would give her just such advice."

"My dear, it isn't a case for advice; it's a case for match-making," reiterated Mrs. Ferguson, as she once more held out her hand.

Meanwhile Miss Durant thoughtfully went down the steps to her carriage, so abstracted from what she was doing that after the footman tucked the fur robe about her feet, he stood waiting for his orders; and finally, realising his mistress's unconsciousness, touched his hat and asked,—

"Where to, Miss Constance?"

With a slight start the girl came back from her meditations, and, after a moment's hesitation, gave a direction. Then, as the man mounted to his seat and the brougham started, the girl's face, which had hitherto been pale, suddenly flushed, and she leaned back in the carriage, so that no one should see her wipe her eyes with her handkerchief.

"I do wish," she murmured, with a slight break in her voice, "that at least mama wouldn't talk about it to outsiders. I—I'd marry to-morrow, just to escape it all—if—if—a loveless marriage wasn't even worse." The girl shivered slightly, and laid her head against the cushioned side, as if weary.

She was still so busy with her thoughts that she failed to notice when the brougham stopped at the florist's, and once more was only recalled to concrete concerns by the footman opening the door. The ordering of some flowers for a débutante evidently steadied her and allowed her to regain self-control, for she drove in succession to the jeweller's to select a wedding gift, and to the dressmaker's for a fitting, at each place giving the closest attention to the matter in hand. These nominal duties, but in truth pleasures, concluded, nominal pleasures, but in truth duties, succeeded them, and the carriage halted at four houses long enough to ascertain that the especial objects of Miss Durant's visits "begged to be excused," or were

- 5 -

"not at home," each of which pieces of information, or, to speak more correctly, the handing in by the footman, in response to the information, of her card or cards, drew forth an unmistakable sigh of relief from that young lady. Evidently Miss Durant was bored by people, and this to those experienced in the world should be proof that Miss Durant was, in fact, badly bored by herself.

One consequence of her escape, however, was that the girl remained with an hour which must be got through with in some manner, and so, in a voice totally without desire or eagerness, she said, "The Park, Wallace;" and in the Park some fifty minutes were spent, her greatest variation from the monotony of the wonted and familiar roads being an occasional nod of the head to people driving or riding, with a glance at those with each, or at the costumes they wore.

It was with a distinct note of anticipation in her voice, therefore, that Miss Durant finally ordered, "Home, now, Murdock;" and, if the truth were to be told, the chill in her hands and feet, due to the keen November cold, with a mental picture of the blazing wood fire of her own room, and of the cup of tea that would be drank in front of it, was producing almost the first pleasurable prospect of the day to her.

Seemingly the coachman was as eager to be in-doors as his mistress, for he whipped up the horses, and the carriage was quickly crossing the plaza and speeding down the avenue. Though the street was crowded with vehicles and pedestrians, the growing darkness put an end to Miss Durant's nods of recognition, and she leaned back, once more buried in her own thoughts.

At Forty-second Street she was sharply recalled from whatever her mind was dwelling upon by a sudden jar, due to the checking of the carriage, and simultaneously with it came the sound of crashing of glass and splintering of wood. So abrupt was the halt that Miss Durant was pitched forward, and as she put out her hand to save herself from being thrown into the bottom of the brougham, she caught a moment's glimpse of a ragged boy close beside her window, and heard, even above the hurly-burly of the pack of carriages and street-crossers, his shrill cry,—

"Extry *Woild'r Joinal.* Terrible—"

There the words ended, for the distraught horses shied backwards and sideways, and the fore wheel, swung outwards by the sharp turn, struck the little fellow and threw him down. Miss Durant attempted a warning cry, but it was too late; and even as it rang out, the carriage gave a jolt and then a jar as it passed over the body. Instantly came a dozen warning shouts and shrieks and curses, and the horses reared and plunged wildly, with the new fright of something under their feet.

White with terror, the girl caught at the handle, but she did no more than throw open the door, for, as if they sprang from the ground, a crowd of men were pressing about the brougham. All was confusion for a moment; then the tangle of vehicles seemed to open out and the mob of people, struggling and gesticulating, fell back before a policeman while another, aided by some one, caught the heads of the two horses, just as the footman drew out from under their feet into the cleared space something which looked like a bundle of rags and newspapers.

Thinking of nothing save that limp little body, Miss Durant sprang out, and kneeling beside it, lifted the head gently into her lap, and smoothed back from the pallid face the unkempt hair. "He isn't dead, Wallace?" she gasped out.

"I don't think he is, Miss Constance, though he looks like he was bad hurt. An', indeed, Miss Constance, it wasn't Murdock's fault. The coupé backed right into our pole without—"

"Here," interrupted a man's voice from the circle of spectators, "give him this;" and some one handed to the girl the cup of a flask half full of brandy. Dipping her fingers into it, she rubbed them across the mouth and forehead; then, raising the head with one of her arms, she parted the lips and poured a few drops between them.

"Now, mum," suggested the policeman. "Just you let go of it, and we'll lift it to where it can stay till the ambulance gets here."

"Oh, don't," begged Miss Durant. "He shouldn't be moved until—"

"Like as not it'll take ten minutes to get it here, and we can't let the street stay blocked like this."

"Ten minutes!" exclaimed the girl. "Isn't it possible—We must get help sooner, or he—" She broke in upon her own words, "Lift him into my carriage, and I'll take him to the hospital."

"Can't let you, miss," spoke up a police sergeant, who meantime had forced his way through the crowd. "Your coachman's got to stay and answer for this."

"He shall, but not now," protested Miss Durant. "I will be responsible for him. Wallace, give them one of my cards from the case in the carriage."

"Miss Durant sprang out and lifted the head gently"

The officer took the bit of pasteboard and looked at it. "That's all right, miss," he said. "Here, Casey, together now and easy."

The two big men in uniform lifted the urchin as if he were without weight, and laid him as gently as might be on the seat of the brougham. This done, the roundsman dropped the small front seat, helped Miss Durant in, and once she was seated upon it, took his place beside her. The sergeant closed the door, gave an order to the coachman, and, wheeling about, the carriage turned up the avenue, followed by the eyes of the crowd and by a trail of the more curious.

"Better give it another swig, mum," counselled her companion; and the girl, going on her knees, raised the head, and administered a second swallow of the brandy. She did not resume her seat, but kept her arm about the boy, in an attempt to render his position easier. It was a wizened, pinched little face she gazed down at, and now the mouth was drawn as if there was physical suffering, even in the unconsciousness. Neither head nor hands had apparently ever known soap, but the dirt only gave picturesqueness, and, indeed, to Miss Durant an added pathos; and the tears came into her eyes as she noted that under the ragged coat was only a flimsy cotton shirt, so bereft of buttons that the whole chest was exposed to the cold which but a little while before the girl, clad in furs and sheltered by the carriage, had yet found so nipping. She raised her free hand and laid it gently on the exposed breast, and slightly shivered as she felt how little warmth there was.

"Please put the fur rug over him," she requested; and her companion pulled it from under their feet, and laid it over the coiled-up legs and body.

The weight, or the second dose of the stimulant, had an effect, for Miss Durant felt the body quiver, and then the eyes unclosed. At first they apparently saw nothing, but slowly the dulness left them, and they, and seemingly the whole face, sharpened into comprehension, and then, as they fastened on the blue coat of the policeman, into the keenest apprehension.

"Say," he moaned, "I didn't do nuttin', dis time, honest."

"I ain't takin' you to the station-house," denied the officer, colouring and looking sideways at his companion.

"You were run over, and we are carrying you to where a doctor can see how much you are hurt," said the gently.

The eyes of the boy turned to hers, and the face lost some of its fright and suspicion. "Is dat on de level?" he asked, after a moment's scrutiny. "Youse oin't runnin' me in?"

"No," answered Miss Durant. "We are taking you to the hospital."

"De horspital!" exclaimed the little chap, his eyes brightening. "Is Ise in de rattler?"

"The what?" asked Constance.

"De rattler," repeated the questioner, "de ding-dong."

"No, you ain't in no ambulance," spoke up the officer. "You're in this young lady's carriage."

The look of hope and pride faded out of the boy's face. "Ise oin't playin' in no sorter luck dese days," he sighed. Suddenly the expression of alarm reappeared in his face. "Wheer's me papes?"

- 9 -

"They're all right. Don't you work yourself up over them," said the roundsman, heartily.

"Youse didn't let de udder newsies swipe dem, did youse?" the lad appealed anxiously.

"I'll pay you for every one you lost," offered Constance. "How many did you have?"

The ragamuffin stared at her for a moment, his face an essence of disbelief.

"Ah, hell!" he ejaculated. "Wot's dis song an' dance youse givin' us?"

"Really, I will," insisted the girl. She reached back of her and took her purse from the rack, and as well as she could with her one hand opened it.

The sight of the bills and coin brought doubt to the sceptic. "Say," he demanded, his eyes burning with avidity, "does youse mean dat? Dere oin't no crawl in dis?"

"No. How much were they worth?"

The boy hesitated, and scanned her face, as if he were measuring the girl more than he was his loss. "Dere wuz twinty *Joinals*," he said, speaking slowly, and his eyes watching her as a cat might a mouse, "an'—an'— twinty *Woilds*—an'—an' tirty *Telegrams*— an'—an'—" He drew a fresh breath, as if needing strength, shot an apprehensive glance at the roundsman, and went on hurriedly, in a lower voice, "an' tirty-five *Posts*—"

"Ah, g'long with you," broke in the policeman, disgustedly. "He didn't have mor'n twenty in all, that I know."

"Hope I may die if Ise didn't have all dem papes, boss," protested the boy.

"You deserve to be run in, that's what you do," asserted the officer of the law, angrily.

"Oh, don't threaten him," begged Miss Durant.

"Don't you be fooled by him, mum. He ain't the kind as sells *Posts*, an' if he was, he wouldn't have more'n five."

"It's de gospel trute Ise chuckin' at youse dis time," asserted the youngster.

"Gospel Ananias—!" began the officer.

"Never mind," interrupted Miss Durant. "Would ten dollars pay for them all?"

"Ah, I know'd youse wuz tryin' to stuff me," dejectedly exclaimed the boy; then, in an evident attempt to save his respect for his own acuteness, he added: "But youse didn't. I seed de goime youse wuz settin' up right from de start."

Out of the purse Constance, with some difficulty, drew a crisp ten-dollar bill, the boy watching the one-handed operation half doubtingly and half eagerly; and when it was finally achieved, at the first movement of her hand toward him, his arm shot out, and the money was snatched, more than taken. With the quick motion, however, the look of eagerness and joy changed to one of agony; he gave a sharp cry, and, despite the grime, the cheeks whitened perceptibly.

"Oh, please stay quiet," implored Miss Durant. "You mustn't move."

"Hully gee, but dat hurted!" gasped the youngster, yet clinging to the new wealth. He lay quiet for a few breaths; then, as if he feared the sight of the bill might in time tempt a change of mind in the giver, he stole the hand to his trousers pocket and endeavoured to smuggle the money into it, his teeth set, but his lips trembling, with the pain the movement cost him.

Not understanding the fear in the boy's mind, Constance put her free hand down and tried to assist him; but the instant he felt her fingers, his tightened violently. "Youse guv it me," he wailed. "Didn't she guv it me?" he appealed desperately to the policeman.

"I'm only trying to help put it in your pocket," explained the girl.

"Ah, chase youseself!" exclaimed the doubter, contemptuously. "Dat don't go wid me. Nah!"

"What doesn't go?" bewilderedly questioned Miss Durant.

"Wotcher tink youse up aginst? Suttin' easy? Well, I guess not! Youse don't get youse pickers in me pocket on dat racket."

"She ain't goin' to take none of your money!" asserted the policeman, indignantly. "Can't you tell a real lady when you see her?"

"Den let her quit tryin' to go tru me," protested the anxious capitalist; and Constance desisted from her misinterpreted attempt, with a laugh which died as the little fellow, at last successful in his endeavour to secrete the money, moaned again at the pain it cost him.

"Shall we never get there?" she demanded impatiently, and, as if an answer were granted her, the carriage slowed, and turning, passed into a porte-cochère, in which the shoes of the horses rang out sharply, and halted.

"Stay quiet a bit, mum," advised the policeman, as he got out; and Constance remained, still supporting the urchin, until two men with a

- 11 -

stretcher appeared, upon which they lifted the little sufferer, who screamed with pain that even this gentlest of handling cost him.

Her heart wrung with sympathy for him, Miss Durant followed after them into the reception-ward. At the door she hesitated, in doubt as to whether it was right or proper for her to follow, till the sight of a nurse reassured her, and she entered; but her boldness carried her no farther than to stand quietly while the orderlies set down the litter. Without a moment's delay the nurse knelt beside the boy, and with her scissors began slitting up the sleeves of the tattered coat.

"Hey! Wotcher up to?" demanded the waif, suspiciously.

"I'm getting you ready for the doctor," said the nurse, soothingly. "It's all right."

"Toin't nuttin' of de sort," moaned the boy. "Youse spoilin' me cloes, an' if youse wuzn't a loidy, you'd get youse face poked in, dat's wot would happen to youse."

Constance came forward and laid her hand on the little fellow's cheek. "Don't mind," she said, "and I'll give you a new suit of clothes."

"Wen?" came the quick question.

"To-morrow."

"Does youse mean dat? Honest? Dere oin't no string to dis?"

"Honest," echoed the girl, heartily.

Reassured, the boy lay quietly while the nurse completed the dismemberment of the ragged coat, the apology for a shirt, and the bit of twine which served in lieu of suspenders. But the moment she began on the trousers, the wail was renewed.

"Quit, I say, or I'll soak de two of youse; see if I don't. Ah, won't youse—" The words became inarticulate howls which the prayers and assurances of the two women could not lessen.

"Now, then, stop this noise and tell me what is the matter," ordered a masculine voice; and turning from the boy, Constance found a tall, strong-featured man with tired-looking eyes standing at the other side of the litter.

Hopeful that the diversion might mean assistance, the waif's howls once more became lingual. "Dey's tryin' to swipe me money, boss," he whined. "Hope I may die if deys oin't."

"And where is your money?" asked the doctor.

- 12 -

"Wotcher want to know for?" demanded the urchin, with recurrent suspicion in his face.

"It's in the pocket of his trousers, Dr. Armstrong," said the nurse.

Without the slightest attempt to reassure the boy, the doctor forced loose the boy's hold on the pocket, and inserting his hand, drew out the ten-dollar bill and a medley of small coins.

"Now," he said, "I've taken your money, so they can't. Understand?"

The urchin began to snivel.

"Ah, you have no right to be so cruel to him," protested Miss Durant. "It's perfectly natural. Just think how we would feel if we didn't understand."

The doctor fumbled for his eye-glasses, but not finding them quickly enough, squinted his eyelids in an endeavour to see the speaker. "And who are you?" he demanded.

"Why, I am—that is—I am Miss Durant, and—" stuttered the girl.

Not giving her time to finish her speech, Dr. Armstrong asked, "Why are you here?" while searching for his glasses.

"I did not mean to intrude," explained Constance, flushing, "only it was my fault, and it hurts me to see him suffer more than seems necessary."

Abandoning the search for his glasses, and apparently unheeding of her explanation, the doctor began a hasty examination of the now naked boy, passing his hand over trunk and limbs with a firm touch that paid no heed to the child's outcries, though each turned the onlooker faint and cold.

Her anxiety presently overcoming the sense of rebuke, the overwrought girl asked, "He will live, won't he?"

The man straightened up from his examination. "Except for some contusion," he replied, "it apparently is only a leg and a couple of ribs broken." His voice and manner conveyed the idea that legs and ribs were but canes and corsets. "Take him into the accident ward," he directed to the orderlies, "and I'll attend to him presently."

"I will not have this boy neglected," Constance said, excitedly and warmly. "Furthermore, I insist that he receive instant treatment, and not wait *your* convenience."

Once again Dr. Armstrong began feeling for his glasses, as he asked, "Are you connected with this hospital, Miss Durant?"

"No, but it was my carriage ran over him, and—"

"And is it because you ran over the boy, Miss Durant," he interrupted, "that you think it is your right to come here and issue instructions for our treatment of him?"

"It is every one's right to see that assistance is given to an injured person as quickly as possible," retorted the girl, though flushing, "and to protest if human suffering, perhaps life itself, is made to wait the convenience of one who is paid to save both."

Finally discovering and adjusting his glasses, Dr. Armstrong eyed Miss Durant with a quality of imperturbability at once irritating and embarrassing. "I beg your pardon for the hasty remark I just made," he apologised. "Not having my second sight at command, I did not realise I was speaking to so young a girl, and therefore I allowed myself to be offended, which was foolish. If you choose to go with the patient, I trust you will satisfy yourself that no one in this hospital is lacking in duty or kindness."

With a feeling much akin to that she had formerly suffered at the conclusion of her youthful spankings, Constance followed hurriedly after the orderlies, only too thankful that a reason had been given her permitting an escape from those steady eyes and amused accents, which she was still feeling when the litter was set down beside an empty bed.

"Has dat slob tooken me money for keeps?" whimpered the boy the moment the orderlies had departed.

"No, no," Constance assured him, her hand in his.

"Den w'y'd he pinch it so quick?"

"He's going to take care of it for you, that's all."

"Will he guv me a wroten pape sayin' dat?"

"See," said the girl, only eager to relieve his anxiety, "here is my purse, and there is a great deal more money in it than you had, and I'll leave it with you, and if he doesn't return you your money, why, you shall have mine."

"Youse cert'in dere's more den Ise had?"

"Certain. Look, here are two tens and three fives and a one, besides some change."

"Dat's all hunky!" joyfully ejaculated the urchin. "Now, den, wheer kin we sneak it so he don't git his hooks on it?"

"This is to be your bed, and let's hide it under the pillow," suggested Constance, feeling as if she were playing a game. "Then you can feel of it whenever you want."

"Dat's de way to steal a base off 'im," acceded the waif. "We'll show dese guys wese oin't no bunch of easy grapes."

Scarcely was the purse concealed when a nurse appeared with a pail of water and rolls of some cloth, and after her came the doctor.

"Now, my boy," he said, with a kindness and gentleness in his voice which surprised Constance, "I've got to hurt you a little, and let's see how brave you can be." He took hold of the left leg the ankle and stretched it, at the same time manipulating the calf with the fingers of his other hand.

The boy gave a cry of pain, and clutched Constance's arm, squeezing it so as to almost make her scream; but she set her teeth determinedly and took his other hand in hers.

At a word the nurse grasped the limb and held it as it was placed, while the doctor took one of the rolls, and, dipping it in the water, unrolled it round and round the leg, with a rapidity and deftness which had, to Constance, a quality of fascination in it. A second wet bandage was wound over the first, then a dry one, and the leg was gently laid back on the litter. "Take his temperature," ordered the doctor, as he began to apply strips of adhesive plaster to the injured ribs; and though it required some persuasion by the nurse and Constance, the invalid finally was persuaded to let the little glass lie under his tongue. His task completed, Dr. Armstrong withdrew the tube and glanced at it.

"Dat medicine oin't got much taste, boss," announced the urchin, cheerfully, "but it soytenly done me lots of good."

The doctor looked up at Constance with a pleasant smile. "There's both the sense and the nonsense of the Christian Science idiocy," he said; and half in response to his smile and half in nervous relief, Constance laughed merrily.

"I am glad for anything that makes him feel better," she replied; then, colouring once more, she added, "and will you let me express my regret for my impulsive words a little while ago, and my thanks to you for relieving the suffering for which I am, to a certain extent, responsible?"

"There is no necessity for either, Miss Durant, though I am grateful for both," he replied.

"Will there be much suffering?"

"Probably no more than ordinarily occurs in such simple fractures," said the doctor; "and we'll certainly do our best that there shall not be."

"And may I see him to-morrow?"

"Certainly, if you come between eleven and one."

"Thank you," said Constance. "And one last favour. Will you tell me the way to my carriage?"

"If you will permit me, I'll see you to it," offered Dr. Armstrong.

With an acknowledgment of the head, Constance turned and took the boy's hand and said a good-bye.

"Do you suppose all newsboys are so dreadfully sharp and suspicious?" she asked of her guide, as they began to descend the stairs, more because she was conscious that he was eyeing her with steady scrutiny than for any other reason.

"I suppose the life is closer to that of the wild beast than anything we have in so-called civilisation. Even a criminal has his pals, but, like the forest animal, everyone—even his own kind—is an enemy to the street waif."

"It must be terrible to suspect and fear even kindness," sighed the girl, with a slight shudder. "I shall try to teach him what it means."

"There does not appear to be any carriage here, Miss Durant," announced her escort.

"Surely there must be. The men can't have been so stupid as not to wait!"

The doctor tapped on the window of the lodge. "Didn't this lady's carriage remain here?" he asked, when the porter had opened it.

"It stayed till the policeman came down, doctor. He ordered it to go to the police-station, and got in it."

"I forgot that my coachman must answer for the accident. Is there a cab-stand near here?"

Dr. Armstrong looked into her eyes, with an amusement which yet did not entirely obliterate the look of admiration, of which the girl was becoming more and more conscious. "The denizens of Avenue A have several cab-stands, of course," he replied, "but they prefer to keep them over on Fifth Avenue."

"It was a foolish question, I suppose" coldly retorted Constance, quite as moved thereto by the scrutiny as by the words, "but I did not even notice where the carriage was driving when we came here. Can you tell me the nearest car line which will take me to Washington Square?"

"As it is five blocks away, and the neighbourhood is not of the nicest, I shall take the liberty of walking with you to it."

"Really, I would rather not. I haven't the slightest fear," protested the girl, eager to escape both the observation and the obligation.

"But I have," calmly said her companion, as if his wish were the only thing to be considered.

For a moment Miss Durant vacillated, then, with a very slight inclination of her head, conveying the smallest quantity of consent and acknowledgment she could express, she walked out of the porte-cochere.

The doctor put himself beside her, and; they turned down the street, but not one word did she say. "If he will force his society upon me, I will at least show him my dislike of it," was her thought.

Obviously Dr. Armstrong was not disturbed by Miss Durant's programme, for the whole distance was walked in silence; and even when they halted on the corner, he said nothing, though the girl was conscious that his eyes still studied her face.

"I will not be the first to speak," she vowed to herself; but minute after minute passed without the slightest attempt or apparent wish on his part, and finally she asked, "Are you sure this line is running?"

Her attendant pointed up the street. "That yellow light is your car. I don't know why the intervals are so long this evening. Usually—"

He was interrupted by the girl suddenly clutching at her dress, and then giving an exclamation of real consternation.

"What is it?" he questioned.

"Why, I—nothing—that is, I think—I prefer to walk home, after all," she stammered.

"You mustn't do that. It's over two miles, and through a really rough district."

"I choose to, none the less," answered Constance, starting across the street.

"Then you will have to submit to my safeguard for some time longer, Miss Durant," asserted the doctor, as he overtook her.

Constance stopped. "Dr. Armstrong," she said, "I trust you will not insist on accompanying me farther, when I tell you I haven't the slightest fear of anything."

"You have no fear, Miss Durant," he answered, "because you are too young and inexperienced to even know the possibilities. This is no part of the city for you to walk alone in after dark. Your wisest course is to take a car, but if you prefer not, you had best let me go with you."

"I choose not to take a car," replied the girl, warmly, "and you have no right to accompany me against my wish."

Dr. Armstrong raised his hat. "I beg your pardon. I did not realize that my presence was not desired," he said.

Angry at both herself and him, Constance merely bowed, and walked on. "I don't see why men have to torment me so," she thought, as she hurried along. "His face was really interesting, and if he only wouldn't begin like— He never would have behaved so if—if I weren't—" Miss Durant checked even her thoughts from the word "beautiful," and allowed the words "well dressed" to explain her magnetism to the other sex. Then, as if to salve her conscience of her own hypocrisy, she added, "It really is an advantage to a girl, if she doesn't want to be bothered by men, to be born plain."

The truth of her thought was brought home to her with unexpected suddenness, for as she passed a strip of sidewalk made light by the glare from a saloon brilliant with gas, a man just coming out of its door stared boldly, and then joined her.

"Ahem!" he said.

The girl quickened her pace, but the intruder only lengthened his.

"Cold night, isn't it, darling?" he remarked, and tried to take her arm.

Constance shrank away from the familiarity with a loathing and fear which, as her persecutor followed, drove her to the curb.

"How dare you?" she burst out, finding he was not to be avoided.

"Now don't be silly, and—"

There the sentence ended, for the man was jerked backwards by the collar, and then shot forward, with a shove, full length into the gutter.

"I feared you would need assistance, Miss Durant, and so took the liberty of following you at a distance," explained Dr. Armstrong, as the cur picked himself up and slunk away.

"You are very— Thank you deeply for your kindness, Dr. Armstrong," gasped the girl, her voice trembling. "I ought to have been guided by your advice and taken the car, but the truth is, I suddenly remembered - that is, I happened to be without any money, and was ashamed to ask you for a loan. Now, if you'll lend me five cents, I shall be most grateful."

"It is said to be a feminine trait never to think of contingencies," remarked the doctor, "and I think, Miss Durant, that your suggested five cents has a tendency in that direction. I will walk with you to Lexington Avenue, which is now your nearest line, and if you still persist then in refusing my escort, I shall insist that you become my debtor for at least a dollar."

"I really need not take you any further than the car, thank you, Dr. Armstrong, for I can get a cab at Twenty-third Street."

It was a short walk to the car line,—too short, indeed, for Miss Durant to express her sense of obligation as she wished,—and she tried, even as she was mounting the steps, to say a last word, but the car swept her away with the sentence half spoken; and with a want of dignity that was not customary in her, she staggered to a seat. Then as she tendered a dollar bill to the conductor, she remarked to herself,—

"Now, that's a man I'd like for a friend, if only he wouldn't be foolish."

At eleven on the following morning, Miss Durant's carriage once more stopped at the hospital door; and, bearing a burden of flowers, and followed by the footman carrying a large basket, Constance entered the ward, and made her way to the waif's bedside.

"Good-morning," she said to Dr. Armstrong, who stood beside the next patient. "How is our invalid doing?"

"Good-morning," responded the doctor, taking the hand she held out. "I think—"

"We's takin' life dead easy, dat's wot wese is," came the prompt interruption from the pillow, in a voice at once youthful yet worn. "Say, dis oin't no lead pipe cinch, oh, no!"

It was a very different face the girl found, for soap and water had worked wonders with it, and the scissors and brush had reduced the tangled shag of hair to order. Yet the ferret eyes and the alert, over-sharp expression were unchanged.

"I've brought you some flowers and goodies," said Miss Durant. "I don't know how much of it will be good for him," she went on to the doctor, apologetically, "but I hope some will do." Putting the flowers on the bed, from the basket she produced in succession two bottles of port, a mould of wine jelly, a jar of orange marmalade, a box of wafers, and a dish of grapes, apples, and bananas.

"Gee! Won't Ise have a hell of a gorge!" joyfully burst out the invalid.

"We'll see about that," remarked Dr. Armstrong, smiling. "He can have all the other things you've brought, in reason, Miss Durant, except the wine. That must wait till we see how much fever he develops to-day,"

"He is doing well?"

"So far, yes."

"That is a great relief to me. And, Dr. Armstrong, in returning your loan to me, will you let me say once again how grateful I am to you for all your kindness, for which I thanked you so inadequately last night? I deserved all that came to me, and can only wonder how you ever resisted saying, 'I told you so.'"

"I have been too often wrong in my own diagnosing to find any satisfaction or triumph in the mistakes of others," said the doctor, as he took the bill the girl held out to him, and, let it be confessed, the fingers that held it, "nor can I regret anything which gave me an opportunity to serve you."

The speaker put an emphasis on the last word, and eyed Miss Durant in a way that led her to hastily withdraw her fingers, and turn away from his unconcealed admiration. It was to find the keen eyes of the urchin observing them with the closest attention; and as she realised it, she coloured, half in embarrassment and half in irritation.

"How is your leg?" she asked, in an attempt to divert the boy's attention and to conceal her own feeling.

"Say. Did youse know dey done it up in plaster, so dat it's stiff as a bat?" responded the youngster, eagerly. "Wish de udder kids could see it, for dey'll never believe it w'en Ise tells 'em. I'll show it to youse if youse want?" he offered, in his joy over the novelty.

"I saw it put on," said Constance. "Don't you remember?"

"Why, cert! Ise remembers now dat—" A sudden change came over the boy's face. "Wheer's dem cloes youse promised me?" he demanded.

"Oh, I entirely forgot—"

"Ah, forgit youse mudder! Youse a peach, oin't youse?" contemptuously broke in the child.

Miss Durant and Dr. Armstrong both burst out laughing.

"Youse t'ink youse a smarty, but Ise know'd de hull time it wuz only a big bluff dat youse wuz tryin' to play on me, an' it didn't go wid me, nah!" went on the youngster, in an aggrieved tone.

"Isn't he perfectly incorrigible?" sighed Constance.

"Ise oin't," denied the boy, indignantly. "Deyse only had me up onct."

With the question the girl had turned to Dr. Armstrong; then, finding his eyes still intently studying her, she once more gave her attention to the waif.

"Really, I did forget them," she asserted. "You shall have a new suit long before you need it."

"Cert'in dat oin't no fake extry youse shoutin'?"

"Truly. How old are you?"

"Wotcher want to know for?" suspiciously asked the boy.

"So I can buy a suit for that age."

"Dat goes. Ise ate."

"And what's your name?"

"Swot."

"What?" exclaimed the girl.

"Nah. Swot," he corrected.

"How do you spell it?"

"Dun'no'. Dat's wot de newsies calls me, 'cause of wot Ise says to de preacher man."

"And what was that?"

"It wuz one of dem religious mugs wot comes Sunday to de Mulberry Park, see, an' dat day he wuz gassin' to us kids 'bout lettin' a guy as had hit youse onct doin' it ag'in; an' w'en he'd pumped hisself empty, he says to me, says he, 'If a bad boy fetched youse a lick on youse cheek, wot would youse do to 'im?' An' Ise says, 'I'd swot 'im in de gob, or punch 'im in de slats,' says I; an' so de swipes calls me by dat noime. Honest, now, oin't dat kinder talk jus' sickenin'?"

"But you must have another name," suggested Miss Durant, declining to commit herself on that question.

"Sure."

"And what is that?"

"McGarrigle."

"And have you no father or mother?"

"Nah."

"Or brothers or sisters?"

"Nah. Ise oin't got nuttin'."

"Where do you live?"

"Ah, rubber!" disgustedly remarked Swot. "Say, dis oin't no police court, see?"

During all these questions, and to a certain extent their cause, Constance had been quite conscious that the doctor was still watching her, and now she once more turned to him, to say, with an inflection of disapproval,—

"When I spoke to you just now, Dr. Armstrong, I did not mean to interrupt you in your duties, and you must not let me detain you from them."

"I had made my morning rounds long before you came, Miss Durant," equably answered the doctor, "and had merely come back for a moment to take a look at one of the patients."

"I feared you were neglecting—were allowing my arrival to interfere with more important matters," replied Miss Durant, frigidly. "I never knew a denser man," she added to herself, again seeking to ignore his presence by giving her attention to Swot. "I should have brought a book with me to-day, to read aloud to you, but I had no idea what kind of a story would interest you. If you know of one, I'll get it and come to-morrow."

"Gee, Ise in it dis time wid bote feet, oin't Ise? Say, will youse git one of de Old Sleuts? Deys de peachiest books dat wuz ever wroten."

"I will, if my bookshop has one, or can get it for me in time."

"There is little chance of your getting it there, Miss Durant," interposed Dr. Armstrong; "but there is a place not far from here where stories of that character are kept; and if it will save you any trouble, I'll gladly get one of them for you."

"I have already overtaxed your kindness," replied Constance, "and so will not trouble you in this."

"It would be no trouble."

"Thank you, but I shall enjoy the search myself."

"Say," broke in the urchin. "Youse ought to let de doc do it. Don't youse see dat he wants to, 'cause he's stuck on youse?"

"Then I'll come to-morrow and read to you, Swot," hastily remarked Miss Durant, pulling her veil over her face. "Good-bye." Without heeding the boy's "Dat's fine," or giving Dr. Armstrong a word of farewell, she went hurrying along the ward, and then downstairs, to her carriage. Yet once within its shelter, the girl leaned back and laughed merrily. "It's perfectly absurd for him to behave so before all the nurses and patients, and he ought to know better. It is to be hoped *that* was a sufficiently broad hint for his comprehension, and that henceforth he won't do it."

Yet it must be confessed that the boy's remark frequently recurred that day to Miss Durant; and if it had no other result, it caused her to devote an amount of thought to Dr. Armstrong quite out of proportion to the length of the acquaintance.

Whatever the inward effect, Miss Durant could discover no outward evidence that Swot's bombshell had moved Dr. Armstrong a particle more than her less pointed attempts to bring to him a realisation that he was behaving in a manner displeasing to her. When she entered the ward the next morning, the doctor was again there, and this time at the waif's bedside, making avoidance of him out of the question. So with a "this-is-my-busy-day" manner, she gave him the briefest of greetings, and then turned to the boy.

"I've brought you some more goodies, Swot, and I found the story," she announced triumphantly.

"Say, youse a winner, dat's wot youse is; oin't she, doc? Wot's de noime?"

Constance held up to him the red and yellow covered tale. *"The Cracksman's Spoil, or Young Sleuth's Double Artifice"* she read out proudly.

"Ah, g'way! Dat oin't no good. Say, dey didn't do a t'ing to youse, did dey?"

"What do you mean?"

"Dey sold youse fresh, dat's wot dey did. De Young Sleut books oin't no good. Dey's nuttin' but a fake extry."

"Oh, dear!" exclaimed Constance, crestfallenly. "It took me the whole afternoon to find it, but I did think it was what you wanted."

"I was sceptical of your being able to get even an approach to newsboy literature, Miss Durant," said Dr. Armstrong, "and so squandered the large sum of a dime myself. I think this is the genuine article, isn't it?" he asked, as he handed to the boy a pamphlet labelled *Old Sleuth on the Trail.*

"Dat's de real t'ing," jubilantly acceded Swot. "Say, oin't de women doisies for havin' bases stole off 'em? Didn't Ise give youse de warm tip to let de doc git it?"

"You should thank him for saving you from my stupid blunder," answered the girl, artfully avoiding all possibility of personal obligation. "Would you like me to read it to you now?"

"Wouldn't Ise, just!"

Still ignoring Dr. Armstrong, Constance took the seat at the bedside, and opening the book, launched into the wildest sea of blood-letting and crime. Yet thrillingly as it began, she was not oblivious to the fact that for some minutes the doctor stood watching her, and she was quite conscious of when he finally moved away, noiselessly as he went. Once he was gone, she was more at her ease; yet clearly her conscience troubled her a little, for in her carriage she again gave expression to some thought by remarking aloud, "It was rude, of course, but if he will behave so, it really isn't my fault."

"Constance took the seat at the bedside"

The gory tale, in true serial style, was "continued" the next and succeeding mornings, to the enthralment of the listener and the amusement of the reader, the latter finding in her occupation as well a convenient reason for avoiding or putting a limit to the doctor's undisguised endeavours to share, if not, indeed, to monopolise, her attention. Even serials, however, have an end, and on the morning of the sixth reading the impossibly shrewd detective successfully put out of existence, or safely incarcerated each one of the numerous scoundrels who had hitherto triumphed over the law, and Constance closed the book.

"Hully gee!" sighed Swot, contentedly. "Say, dat Old Sleut, he's up to de limit, oin't he? It don't matter wot dey does, he works it so's de hull push comes his way, don't he?"

"He certainly was very far-seeing," Constance conceded; "but what a pity it is that he—that he wasn't in some finer calling."

"Finer wot?"

"How much nobler it would have been if, instead of taking life, he had been saving it—like Dr. Armstrong, for instance," she added, to bring her idea within the comprehension of the boy.

"Ah, dat's de talk for religious mugs an' goils," contemptuously exclaimed the waif, "but it guv's me de sore ear. It don't go wid me, not one little bit."

"Aren't you grateful to Dr. Armstrong for all he's done for you?"

"Bet youse life," assented Swot; "but Ise oin't goin' to be no doctor, nah! Ise goin' to git on de force, dat's de racket Ise outer. Say, will youse read me anudder of dem stories?"

"Gladly, if I can find the right kind this time."

The boy raised his head to look about the ward. "Hey, doc," called his cracked treble.

"Hush, don't!" protested the girl.

"W'y not?"

Before she could frame a reason, the doctor was at the bedside. "What is it?" he asked.

"Say, wese got tru wid dis story, an' Miss Constance says she'll read me anudder, but dey'll set de goime up on her, sure, she bein' a goil; so will youse buy de real t'ing?"

"That I will."

"Dat's hunky." Then he appealed to Constance. "Say, will youse pay for it?" he requested.

"And why should she?" inquired Dr. Armstrong.

- 25 -

"'Cause she's got de dough, an Ise heard de nurse loidies talkin' 'bout youse, an' dey said dat youse wuz poor."

It was the doctor's turn to colour, and flush he did.

"Swot and I will both be very grateful, Dr. Armstrong, if you will get us another of the Old Sleuth books," spoke up Miss Durant, hastily.

"Won't youse guv 'im de price?" reiterated the urchin.

"Then we'll expect it to-morrow morning," went on the girl; and for the first time in days she held out her hand to Dr. Armstrong, "And thank you in advance for your kindness. Good-morning."

"Rats!" she heard, as she walked away. "I didn't tink she'd do de grand sneak like dat, doc, jus' 'cause I tried to touch her for de cash."

Constance slowed one step, then resumed her former pace. "He surely—Of course he'll understand why I hurried away," she murmured.

Blind as he might be, Dr. Armstrong was not blind to the geniality of Miss Durant's greeting the next morning, or the warmth of her thanks for the cheap-looking dime novel. She chatted pleasantly with him some moments before beginning on the new tale; and even when she at last opened the book, there was a subtle difference in the way she did it that made it include instead of exclude him from a share in the reading. And this was equally true of the succeeding days.

The new doings of Old Sleuth did not achieve the success that the previous ones had. The invalid suddenly developed both restlessness and inattention, with such a tendency to frequent interruptions as to make reading well-nigh impossible.

"Really, Swot," Constance was driven to threaten one morning, when he had broken in on the narrative for the seventh time with questions which proved that he was giving no heed to the book, "unless you lie quieter, and don't interrupt so often, I shall not go on reading."

"Dat goes," acceded the little fellow; yet before she had so much as finished a page he asked, "Say, did youse ever play craps?"

"No," she answered, with a touch of severity.

"It's a jim dandy goime, Ise tells youse. Like me to learn youse?"

"No," replied the girl, as she closed the book.

"Goils never oin't no good," remarked Swot, discontentedly.

Really irritated, Miss Durant rose and adjusted her boa. "Swot," she said, "you are the most ungrateful boy I ever knew, and I'm not merely not going to read any more to-day, but I have a good mind not to come to-morrow, just to punish you."

"Ah, chase youseself!" was the response. "Youse can't pass dat gold brick on me, well, I guess!"

"What are you talking about?" indignantly asked Constance.

"Tink Ise oin't onter youse curves? Tink Ise don't hear wot de nurse loidies says? Gee! Ise know w'y youse so fond of comin' here."

"Why do I come here?" asked Constance, in a voice full of warning.

The tone was wasted on the boy.

"'Cause youse dead gone on de doc."

"I am sorry you don't know better than to talk like that, Swot," said the girl, quietly, "because I wanted to be good to you, and now you have put an end to my being able to be. You will have to get some one else to read to you after this. Good-bye." She passed her hand kindly over his forehead, and turned to find that Dr. Armstrong was standing close behind her, and must have overheard more or less of what had been said. Without a word, and looking straight before her, Constance walked away.

Once out of the hospital, her conscience was not altogether easy; and though she kept away the next day, she sent her footman with the usual gift of fruits and other edibles; and this she did again on the morning following.

"Of course he didn't mean to be so atrociously impertinent," she sighed, in truth missing what had come to be such an amusing and novel way of using up some of each twenty-four hours. "But I can't, in self-respect, go to him any more."

These explanations were confided to her double in the mirror, as she eyed the effect of a new gown, donned for a dinner; and while she still studied the eminently satisfactory total, she was interrupted by a knock at the door, and her maid brought her a card the footman handed in.

Constance took it, looked astonished, then frowned slightly, and finally glanced again in the mirror. Without a word, she took her gloves and fan from the maid, and descended to the drawing-room.

"Good-evening, Dr. Armstrong," she said, coolly.

"I have come here—I have intruded on you, Miss Durant," awkwardly and hurriedly began the doctor, "because nothing else would satisfy Swot McGarrigle. I trust you will understand that I—He—he is to undergo an operation, and—well, I told him it was impossible, but he still begged me so to ask you, that I hadn't the heart to refuse him."

"'I have come here—I have intruded on you, Miss Durant,' hurriedly began the doctor"

"An operation!" cried Constance.

"Don't be alarmed. It's really nothing serious. He—Perhaps you may have noticed how restless and miserable he has been lately. It is due, we have decided, to one of the nerves of the leg having been lacerated, and so I am going to remove it, to end the suffering, which is now pretty keen."

"Oh, I'm so sorry," exclaimed the girl, regretfully. "I didn't dream of it, and so was hard on him, and said I wouldn't come any more."

"He has missed your visits very much, Miss Durant, and we found it very hard to comfort him each morning, when only your servant came."

"Has he really? I thought they were nothing to him."

"If you knew that class better, you would appreciate that they are really grateful and warm-hearted, but they fear to show their feelings, and, besides, could not express them, even if they had the words, which they don't. But if you could hear the little chap sing your praises to the nurses and to me, you would not think him heartless. 'My loidy' is his favourite description of you."

"He wants to see me?" questioned the girl, eagerly.

"Yes. Like most of the poorer class, Miss Durant," explained the doctor, "he has a great dread of the knife. To make him less frantic, I promised that I would come to you with his wish; and though I would not for a moment have you present at the actual operation, if you could yield so far as to come to him for a few minutes, and assure him that we are going to do it for his own good, I think it will make him more submissive."

"When do you want me?" asked Miss Durant.

"It is—I am to operate as soon as I can get back to the hospital, Miss Durant. It has been regrettably postponed as it is."

The girl stood hesitating for a moment. "But what am I to do about my dinner?"

Dr. Armstrong's eyes travelled over her from head to foot, taking in the charming gown of satin and lace, the strings of pearls about her exquisite throat and wrists, and all the other details which made up such a beautiful picture. "I forgot," he said, quietly, "that society duties now take precedence over all others." Then, with an instant change of manner, he went on: "You do yourself an injustice, I think, Miss Durant, in even questioning what you are going to do. You know you are coming to the boy."

For the briefest instant the girl returned his intent look, trying to fathom what enabled him to speak with such absolute surety; then she said, "Let us lose no time," as she turned back into the hall and hurried out of the front door, not even attending to the doctor's protest about her going without a wrap; and she only said to him at the carriage door, "You will drive with me, of course, Dr. Armstrong?" Then to the footman, "Tell Murdock, the hospital, Maxwell, but you are to go at once to Mrs. Purdy, and say I shall be prevented from coming to her to-night by a call that was not to be disregarded,"

"It was madness of you, Miss Durant, to come out without a cloak, and I insist on your wearing this," said the doctor, the moment the carriage had started, as he removed his own overcoat.

"Oh, I forgot—but I mustn't take it from you, Dr. Armstrong."

"Have no thought of me. I am twice as warmly clad as you, and am better protected than usual."

Despite her protest he placed it about Constance's shoulders and buttoned it up. "You know," he said, "the society girl with her bare throat and arms is at once the marvel and the despair of us doctors, for every dinner or ball ought to have its death-list from pneumonia; but it never—"

"Will it be a very painful operation?" asked the girl.

"Not at all; and the anaesthetic prevents consciousness. If Swot were a little older, I should not have had to trouble you. It is a curious fact that boys, as a rule, face operations more bravely than any other class of patient we have."

"I wonder why that is?" queried Constance.

"It is due to the same ambition which makes cigarette-smokers of them—a desire to be thought manly."

Once the carriage reached the hospital, Constance followed the doctor up the stairs and through the corridor. "Let me relieve you of the coat, Miss Durant," he advised, and took it from her and passed it over to one of the orderlies. Then, opening a door, he made way for her to enter.

"The two were quickly seated on the floor"

Constance passed into a medium-sized room, which a first glance showed her to be completely lined with marble; but there her investigations ceased, for her eyes rested on the glass table upon which lay the little fellow, while beside him stood a young doctor and a nurse. At the sound of her footsteps the boy turned his head till he caught sight of her, when, after an instant's stare, he surprised the girl by hiding his eyes and beginning to cry.

"Ise knowed all along youse wuz goin' to kill me," he sobbed.

"Why, Swot," cried Constance, going to his side. "Nobody is going to kill you."

The hands were removed from the eyes, and still full of tears, they blinkingly stared a moment at the girl.

"Hully gee! Is dat youse?" he ejaculated. "Ise tought youse wuz de angel come for me."

"You may go many years in society, Miss Durant, without winning another compliment so genuine," remarked Dr. Armstrong, smiling. "Nor is it surprising that he was misled," he added.

Constance smiled in return as she answered, "And it only proves how the value of a compliment is not in its truthfulness, but in its being truth to the one who speaks it."

"Say, youse won't let dem do nuttin' bad to me, will youse?" implored the boy.

"They are only going to help you, Swot," the girl assured him, as she took his hand.

"Den w'y do dey want to put me to sleep for?"

"To spare you suffering,"

"Dis oin't no knock-out drops, or dat sorter goime? Honest?"

"No. I won't let them do you any harm."

"Will youse watch dem all de time dey's doin' tings to me?"

"Yes. And if you'll be quiet and take it nicely, I'll bring you a present to-morrow."

"Dat's grand! Wot'll youse guv me? Say, don't do dat," he protested, as the nurse applied the sponge and cone to his face.

"Lie still, Swot," said Constance, soothingly, "and tell me what you would best like me to give you. Shall it be a box of building-blocks—or some soldiers—or a fire-engine—or—"

"Nah. Ise don't want nuttin' but one ting—an' dat's—wot wuz Ise tinkin'—Ise forgits wot it wuz—lemme see—Wot's de matter? Wheer is youse all?—" The little frame relaxed and lay quiet.

"That is all you can do for us, Miss Durant," said Dr. Armstrong.

"May I not stay, as I promised him I would?" begged Constance.

"Can you bear the sight of blood?"

"I don't know—but see—I'll turn my back." Suiting the action to the word, the girl faced so that, still holding Swot's hand, she was looking away from the injured leg.

A succession of low-spoken orders to his assistants was the doctor's way of telling her that he left her to do as she chose, She stood quietly for a few minutes, but presently her desire to know the progress of the operation, and her anxiety over the outcome, proved too strong for her, and she turned her head to take a furtive glance. She did not look away again, but with a strange mixture of fascination and squeamishness, she watched as the bleeding was stanched with sponges, each artery tied, and each muscle drawn aside, until finally the nerve was reached and removed; and she could not but feel both wonder and admiration as she noted how Dr. Armstrong's hands, at other times seemingly so much in his way, now did their work so skilfully and rapidly. Not till the operation was over, and the resulting wound was being sprayed with antiseptics, did the girl realize how cold and faint she felt, or how she was trembling. Dropping the hand of the boy, she caught at the operating-table, and then the room turned black.

"It's really nothing," she asserted. "I only felt dizzy for an instant. Why! Where am I?"

"You fainted away, Miss Durant, and we brought you here," explained the nurse, once again applying the salts. The woman rose and went to the door. "She is conscious now, Dr. Armstrong."

As the doctor entered Constance tried to rise, but a motion of his hand checked her. "Sit still a little yet, Miss Durant," he ordered peremptorily. From a cupboard he produced a plate of crackers and a glass of milk, and brought them to her.

"I really don't want anything," declared the girl.

"You are to eat something at once," insisted Dr. Armstrong, in a very domineering manner.

He held the glass to her lips, and Constance, after a look at his face, took a swallow of the milk, and then a piece of cracker he broke off.

"How silly of me to behave so," she said, as she munched.

"The folly was mine in letting you stay in the room when you had had no dinner. That was enough to knock up any one," answered the doctor. "Here." Once again the glass was held to her lips, and once again, after a look at his face, Constance drank, and then accepted a second bit of cracker from his fingers.

"Do you keep these especially for faint-minded women?" she asked, trying to make a joke of the incident.

"This is my particular sanctum, Miss Durant; and as I have a reprehensible habit of night-work, I keep them as a kind of sleeping potion."

Constance glanced about the room with more interest, and as she noticed the simplicity and the bareness, Swot's remark concerning the doctor's poverty came back to her. Only many books and innumerable glass bottles, a microscope, and other still more mysterious instruments, seemed to save it from the tenement-house, if not, indeed, the prison, aspect.

"Are you wondering how it is possible for any one to live in such a way?" asked the doctor, as his eyes followed hers about the room.

"If you will have my thought," answered Constance, "it was that I am in the cave of the modern hermit, who, instead of seeking solitude, because of the sins of mankind, seeks it that he may do them good."

"We have each had a compliment to-night," replied Dr. Armstrong, his face lighting up.

The look in his eyes brought something into the girl's thoughts, and with a slight effort she rose. "I think I am well enough now to relieve you of my intrusion," she said.

"You will not be allowed to leave the hermit's cell till you have finished the cracker and the milk," affirmed the man. "I only regret that I can't keep up the character by offering you locusts and wild honey."

"At least don't think it necessary to stay here with me," said Miss Durant, as she dutifully began to eat and drink again. "If—oh—the operation— How is Swot?"

"Back in the ward, though not yet conscious."

"And the operation?"

"Absolutely successful."

"Despite my interruption?"

"Another marvel to us M.D.'s is the way so sensitive a thing as a woman will hold herself in hand by sheer nerve force when it is necessary. You did not faint till the operation was completed."

"Now may I go?" asked the girl, with a touch of archness, as she held up the glass and the plate, both empty.

"Yes, if you will let me share your carriage. Having led you into this predicament, the least I feel I can do is to see you safely out of it."

"Now the hermit is metamorphosing himself into a knight," laughed Constance, merrily, "with a distressed damsel on his hands. I really need not put you to the trouble, but I shall be glad if you will take me home."

- 34 -

Once again the doctor put his overcoat about her, and they descended the stairs and entered the brougham.

"Tell me the purpose of all those instruments I saw in your room," she asked as they started.

"They are principally for the investigation of bacteria. Not being ambitious to spend my life doctoring whooping-cough and indigestion, I am striving to make a scientist of myself."

"Then that is why you prefer hospital work?"

"No. I happen to have been born with my own living to make in the world, and when I had worked my way through the medical school, I only too gladly became 'Interne' here, not because it is what I wish to do, but because I need the salary."

"Yet it seems such a noble work."

"Don't think I depreciate it, but what I am doing is only remedial What I hope to do is to prevent."

"How is it possible?"

"For four years my every free hour has been given to studying what is now called tuberculosis, and my dream is to demonstrate that it is in fact the parent disease—a breaking down—disintegration—of the bodily substance—the tissue, or cell—and to give to the world a specific."

"How splendid!" exclaimed Constance. "And you believe you can?"

"Every day makes me more sure that both demonstration and specific are possible —but it is unlikely that I shall be the one to do it."

"I do not see why?"

"Because there are many others studying the disease who are free from the necessity of supporting themselves, and so can give far more time and money to the investigation than is possible for me. Even the scientist must be rich in these days, Miss Durant, if he is to win the great prizes."

"Won't you tell me something about yourself?" requested Constance, impulsively.

"There really is nothing worth while yet. I was left an orphan young, in the care of an uncle who was able to do no better for me than to get me a place in a drug-store. By doing the night-work it was possible to take the course at the medical college; and as I made a good record, this position was offered to me."

"It—you could make it interesting if you tried."

- 35 -

"I'm afraid I am not a realist, Miss Durant. I dream of a future that shall be famous by the misery and death I save the world from, but my past is absolutely eventless."

As he ended, the carriage drew up at the house, and the doctor helped her out.

"You will take Dr. Armstrong back to the hospital, Murdock," she ordered.

"Thank you, but I really prefer a walk before going to *my* social intimates, the bacilli," answered the doctor, as he went up the steps with her. Then, after he had rung the bell, he held out his hand and said: "Miss Durant, I need scarcely say, after what I have just told you, that my social training has been slight—so slight that I was quite unaware that the old adage, 'Even a cat may look at a king,' was no longer a fact until I overheard what was said the other day. My last wish is to keep you from coming to the hospital, and in expressing my regret at having been the cause of embarrassment to you, I wish to add a pledge that henceforth, if you will resume your visits, you and Swot shall be free from my intrusion. Good-night," he ended, as he started down the steps.

"But I never—really I have no right to exclude—nor do I wish—" protested the girl; and then, as the servant opened the front door, even this halting attempt at an explanation ceased. She echoed a "Good-night," adding, "and thank you for all your kindness," and very much startled and disturbed the footman, as she passed into the hallway, by audibly remarking, "Idiot!"

She went upstairs slowly, as if thinking, and once in her room, seated herself at her desk and commenced a note. Before she had written a page she tore the paper in two and began anew. Twice she repeated this proceeding; then rose in evident irritation, and, walking to her fire, stood looking down into the flame. "I'll think out what I had better do when I'm not so tired," she finally remarked, as she rang for her maid. But once in bed, her thoughts, or the previous strain, kept her long hours awake; and when at last she dropped into unconsciousness her slumber was made miserable by dreams mixing in utter confusion operating-room and dinner, guests and microbes—dreams in which she was alternately striving to explain something to Dr. Armstrong, who could not be brought to understand, or to conceal something he was determined to discover. Finally she found herself stretched on the dinner-table, the doctor, knife in hand, standing over her, with the avowed intention of opening her heart to learn some secret, and it was her helpless protests and struggles which brought consciousness to her—to discover that she had slept far into the morning.

With the one thought of a visit to the hospital during the permitted hours, she made a hasty toilet, followed by an equally speedy breakfast, and was actually on her way downstairs when she recalled her promise of a gift. A glance at her watch told her that there was not time to go to the shops, and hurrying back to her room, she glanced around for something among the knick-knacks scattered about. Finding nothing that she could conceive of as bringing pleasure to the waif, she took from a drawer of her desk a photograph of herself, and descended to the carriage.

She had reason to be thankful for her recollection, as, once her greetings, and questions to the nurse about the patient's condition were made, Swot demanded,

"Wheer's dat present dat youse promised me?"

"I did not have time this morning to get something especially for you," she explained, handing him the portrait, "so for want of anything better, I've brought you my picture."

The urchin took the gift and looked at both sides. "Wotinell's dat good for?" he demanded contemptuously.

"I thought—hoped it might please you, as showing you that I had forgiven—that I liked you."

"Ah, git on de floor an' look at youseself," disgustedly remarked Swot. "Dat talk don't cut no ice wid me. W'y didn't youse ask wot Ise wants?"

"And what would you like?"

"Will youse guv me a pistol?"

"Why, what would you do with it?"

"I'd trow a scare into de big newsies w'en dey starts to chase me off de good beats."

"Really, Swot, I don't think I ought to give you anything so dangerous. You are very young to—"

"Ah! Youse a goil, an' deyse born frightened. Bet youse life, if youse ask de doc, he won't tink it nuttin' to be scared of."

"He isn't here this morning," remarked Constance, for some reason looking fixedly at the glove she was removing as she spoke.

The urchin raised his head and peered about. "Dat's funny!" he exclaimed. "It's de first time he oin't bin here w'en youse wuz at de bat."

"Has he seen you this morning?"

- 37 -

"Why, cert!"

The girl opened the dime novel and found the page at which the interruption had occurred, hesitated an instant, and remarked, "The next time he comes you might say that I would like to see him for a moment—to ask if I had better give you a pistol." This said, she hastily began on the book. Thrillingly as the pursuits and pursuit of the criminal classes were pictured, however, there came several breaks in the reading; and had any keenly observant person been watching Miss Durant, he would have noticed that these pauses invariably happened whenever some one entered the ward.

It was made evident to her that she and Swot gave value to entirely different parts of her message to the doctor; for, no sooner did she reach the waif's bedside the next morning than the invalid announced,—

"Say, Ise done my best to jolly de doc, but he stuck to it dat youse oughtn't to guv me no pistol."

"Didn't you tell him what I asked you to say?" demanded Constance, anxiously.

"Soytenly. Ise says to 'im dat youse wanted to know wot he tought, an' he went back on me. Ise didn't tink he'd trun me down like dat!"

"I might better have written him," murmured Miss Durant, thoughtfully. She sat for some time silently pondering, till the waif asked,—

"Say, youse goin' to guv me dat present just de same, oin't youse?"

"Yes, I'll give you a present," acceded the girl, opening the book. "I think, Swot," she continued, "that we'll have to trouble Dr. Armstrong for another Old Sleuth, as we shall probably finish this to-day. And tell him this time it is my turn to pay for it," From her purse she produced a dime, started to give it to the boy, hastily drew back her hand, and replacing the coin, substituted for it a dollar bill. Then she began reading rapidly—so rapidly that the end of the story was attained some twenty minutes before the visitors' time had expired.

"Say," was her greeting on the following day, as Swot held up another lurid-looking tale and the dollar bill, "Ise told de doc youse wuzn't willin' dat he, bein' poor, should bleed de cash dis time, an' dat youse guv me dis to—"

"You didn't put it that way, Swot?" demanded Miss Durant.

"Wot way?"

"That I said he was poor."

"Soytenly."

"Oh, Swot, how could you?"

"Wot's de matter?"

"I never said that! Was he—was he—What did he say?"

"Nuttin' much, 'cept dat I wuz to guv youse back de dough, for de books wuz on 'im."

"I'm afraid you have pained him, Swot, and you certainly have pained me. Did he seem hurt or offended?"

"Nop."

"I wish you would tell him I shall be greatly obliged if he will come to the ward to-morrow, for I wish to see him. Now don't alter this message, please, Swot."

That her Mercury did her bidding more effectively was proved by her finding the doctor at the bedside when she arrived the next day.

"Swot told me that you wished to see me, Miss Durant," he said.

"Yes, and I'm very much obliged to you for waiting. I—How soon will it be possible for him to be up?"

"He is doing so famously that we'll have him out of bed by Monday, I hope."

"I promised him a present, and I want to have a Christmas tree for him, if he can come to it."

"Wot's dat?" came the quick question from the bed.

"If you don't know, I'm going to let it be a surprise to you, Swot. Do you think he will be well enough to come to my house? Of course I'll send my carriage."

"If he continues to improve, he certainly will be."

"Say, is dat de ting dey has for de mugs wot goes to Sunday-school, an' dat dey has a party for?"

"Yes, only this tree will be only for you, Swot,"

"Youse oin't goin' to have no udder swipes but me?"

"No."

"Den who'll git all de presents wot's on de tree?" inquired Swot, suggestively.

"Guess!" laughed Constance.

"Will dey all be for me?"

"Yes."

"Hully gee! But dat's grand! Ise in it up to de limit, doc, oin't Ise?" exclaimed the waif, turning to the doctor.

Dr. Armstrong smiled and nodded his head, but something in his face or manner seemed to give a change to the boy's thoughts, for, after eyeing him intently, he said to Constance,—

"Oin't youse goin' to invite de doc?"

Miss Durant coloured as she said, with a touch of eagerness yet shyness, "Dr. Armstrong, I intended to ask you, and it will give me a great deal of pleasure if you will come to Swot's and my festival." And when the doctor seemed to hesitate, she added, "Please!" in a way that would have very much surprised any man of her own circle.

"Thank you, Miss Durant; I'll gladly come, if you are sure I sha'n't be an interloper."

"Not at all," responded the girl. "On the contrary, it would be sadly incomplete without you—"

"Say," broke in the youngster, "growed-up folks don't git tings off de tree, does dey?"

Both Constance and the doctor laughed at the obvious fear in the boy's mind.

"No, Swot," the man replied; "and I've had my Christmas gift from Miss Durant already."

"Wot wuz dat?"

"Ask her," replied Dr. Armstrong, as he walked away.

"Wot have youse guv 'im?"

Constance laughed, and blushed still more deeply, as, after a slight pause, she replied, "It's my turn, Swot, to say 'rubber'?" This said, she stooped impulsively and kissed the boy's forehead. "You are a dear, Swot," she asserted, warmly.

With the mooting of the Christmas tree, the interest in Old Sleuth markedly declined, being succeeded by innumerable surmises of the rapidly convalescing boy as to the probable nature and number of the gifts it would bear. In this he was not discouraged by Miss Durant, who, once the readings were discontinued, brought a bit of fancy-work for occupation.

"Wot's dat?" he inquired, the first time she produced it.

"A case for handkerchiefs."

"For me?"

"Did you ever have a handkerchief?"

"Nop. An' I'd radder have suttin' else."

"Can you keep a secret, Swot?"

"Bet youse life."

"This is for Dr. Armstrong."

Swot regarded it with new interest. "Youse goin' to s'prise 'im?"

"Yes."

"Den youse must sneak it quick w'en he comes in."

"Haven't you noticed that he doesn't come here any longer, Swot?" quietly responded the girl, her head bowed over the work.

"Oin't dat luck!"

"Why?" asked Constance, looking up in surprise.

"'Cause youse can work on de present," explained Swot. "Say," he demanded after a pause, "if dere's anyting on de tree dat Ise don't cares for, can Ise give it to de doc?"

"Certainly. Or better still, if you'll find out what he would like, I'll let you make him a present."

"Youse payin' for it?" anxiously questioned the boy.

"Of course."

"Dat's Jim Dandy!"

Miss Durant recurred to this offer twice in the succeeding week, but to her surprise, found Swot's apparent enthusiasm over the gift had entirely cooled, and his one object was a seeming desire to avoid all discussion of it.

"Don't you want to give him something, or haven't you found out what he wants?" she was driven to ask.

"Oh, dat's all right. Don't youse tire youself 'bout dat," was his mysterious reply. Nor could she extract anything more satisfactory.

It was a very different Swot McGarrigle who was helped into Miss Durant's carriage by the doctor on Christmas eve from the one who had been lifted out at the hospital some six weeks before. The wizened face had filled out into roundness, and the long-promised new clothes, donned for the first time in honor of the event, even more transformed him; so changed him, in fact, that Constance hesitated for an instant in her welcome, in doubt if it were he.

"I have the tree in my own room, because I wanted all the fun to ourselves," she explained, as she led the way upstairs, "and downstairs we should almost certainly be interrupted by callers, or something. But before you go, Dr. Armstrong, I want you to meet my family, and of course they all want to see Swot."

It was not a large nor particularly brilliant tree, but to Swot it was everything that was beautiful. At first he was afraid to approach, but after a little Constance persuaded him into a walk around it, and finally tempted him, by an artful mention of what was in one of the larger packages at the base, to treat it more familiarly. Once the ice was broken, the two were quickly seated on the floor, Constance cutting strings, and Swot giving shouts of delight at each new treasure. Presently, in especial joy over some prize, the boy turned to show it to the doctor, to discover that he was standing well back, watching, rather than sharing, in the pleasure of the two; and, as the little chap discovered the aloofness, he leaned over and whispered something to the girl.

"I want to, but can't get the courage yet," whispered back Constance. "I don't know what is the matter with me, Swot," she added, blushing.

"Like me to guv it to 'im?"

"Oh, will you, Swot?" she eagerly demanded. "It's the parcel in tissue-paper on my desk over there."

The waif rose to his feet and trotted to the place indicated. He gave a quick glance back at Miss Durant, and seeing that she was leaning over a bundle, he softly unfolded the tissue-paper, slipped something from his newly possessed breast pocket into the handkerchief-case, and refolded the paper. He crossed the room to where the doctor was standing, and handed him the parcel, with the remark, "Dat's for youse, from Miss Constance an' me, doc." Then scurrying back to the side of the girl, he confided to her, "Ise guv de doc a present, too."

"What was it?" asked Constance, still not looking up.

"Go an' ask 'im," chuckled Swot.

Turned away as she might be, she was not unconscious of the doctor's movements, and she was somewhat puzzled when, instead of coming to her with thanks, he crossed the room to a bay-window, where he was hidden by the tree from both of them. From that point he still further astonished her by the request,—

"Can you—will you please come here for a moment, Miss Durant?"

Constance rose and walked to where he stood. "I hope you like my gift?" she asked.

"You could have given me nothing I have so wanted—nothing I shall treasure more," said the man, speaking low and fervently. "But did you realise what this would mean to me?" As he spoke, he raised his hand, and Constance saw, not the handkerchief-case, but a photograph of herself.

"Oh!" she gasped. "Where—I didn't—that was a picture I gave to Swot. The case is my gift,"

The doctor's hand dropped, and all the hope and fire went from his eyes. "I beg your pardon for being so foolish, Miss Durant. I—I lost my senses for a moment—or I would have known that you never—that the other was your gift." He stooped to pick it up from the floor where he had dropped it. "Thank you very deeply for your kindness, and—and try to forget my folly."

"I—I—couldn't understand why Swot suddenly—why he—I never dreamed of his doing it," faltered the girl.

"His and my knowledge of social conventions are about on a par," responded the man, with a set look to his mouth. "Shall I give it back to him or to you?"

Constance drew a deep breath. "It wasn't—my—gift—but—but—I don't mind your keeping it if you wish."

"You mean—?" cried Dr. Armstrong, incredulously.

"Oh," said the girl, hurriedly, "isn't that enough, now? Please, oh, please— wait—for a little."

The doctor caught her hand and kissed it. "Till death, if you ask it!" he said.

Five minutes later Swot abstracted himself sufficiently from his gifts to peep around the tree and ecstatically inquire,—

"Say, oin't dis de doisiest Christmas dat ever wuz?"

"Yes," echoed the two in the bay-window.

"Did youse like me present, doc?"

- 43 -

"Yes," reiterated the doctor, with something in his voice that gave the word tenfold meaning.

"Ise tought youse 'ud freeze to it, an' it wuzn't no sorter good to me."

Constance laughed happily. "Still, I'm very glad I gave it to you, Swot," she said, with a glance of the eyes, half shy and half arch, at the man beside her.

"Did youse like Miss Constance's present too, doc?"

"Yes," replied the doctor, "especially the one you haven't seen, Swot."

"Wot wuz dat?"

"A something called hope—which is the finest thing in the world."

"No. There is one thing better," said Miss Durant.

"What is it?"

"Love!" whispered Constance, softly.

www.ingramcontent.com/pod-product-compliance
Ingram Content Group UK Ltd.
Pitfield, Milton Keynes, MK11 3LW, UK
UKHW040733190225
455309UK00004B/272